MY FAVOURITE TEACHER (NOT) AND OTHER POEMS

MY FAVOURITE TEACHER (NOT) AND OTHER POEMS

TIM PORTER

GINGER CAT BOOKS

Date of Publication:
January 2003

Published by:
Ginger Cat Books
First Published by: Minerva Press 2001

© Copyright Tim Porter 2003

Illustrated by: Neil Chapman

Printed by:
ProPrint
Riverside Cottage
Great North Road
Stibbington
Peterborough PE8 6LR

ISBN: 0-9543980-0-9

CONTENTS

Tracey	1
Thoughts in the Dentist's Waiting Room	3
Trevor Jones	4
Wellington	7
The School Photograph	8
The School Photograph	10
My Favourite Teacher (Not)	13
Please Come Home Mum	14
January	16
The Crocodile	17
Looking After Next Door's Cats While They Are On Holiday	18
Today Down My Street . . .	20
Christmas Joy	21
Henrietta Henry	23
You're Not Going Out Dressed Like That!	25
School Report	26
Detention!	28
The School Nurse is Coming Today	30
Napoleon	32
Half-Time	33
The Elephant and the Engineer	34
The Creature	37
The New Boy	38
Wizzelda Witch	41
Steven Station	42
The Hunt	43
Mr Snail	44
Stray	45
Life's a Spot on Your Nose	47
I Learnt to Swim at the Municipal Baths	48
Why?	49
The Modern Witch	51
Ship Ahoy!	53
Monday, 9.15am	54
Anger	55

TRACEY

I've brought my girlfriend home for tea
But Mum clearly doesn't approve,
She thinks that Tracey's not good enough,
Mum just isn't in the groove.

Just 'cos her body's pierced
In seventeen different places,
Her lipstick's black, her head's been shaved
And her jeans are kept up with braces.

Trace likes to go kick-boxing,
But isn't violent as a rule,
And she offers to show her tattoos off
If Mum'll sit down on the stool.

Meanwhile Dad's trying to be trendy,
He's really trying his best,
In his flares, built-up platform shoes
And his tight fluorescent vest.

He hums along to Oasis
And says he likes The Verve,
But really he listens to The Beatles,
He hasn't half got a nerve.

Next Mum really tries to spoil things
With her tea-time sabotage,
Which is wormy spaghetti bolognaise
And the portions are very large.

No one can eat spaghetti bolognaise
Keeping their manners at their best,
There's lots of slurps and splashes and spills,
And Dad gets it down his vest.

So Mum's made her as welcome as measles,
And next she starts to dig and enquire
About the rest of Tracey's family,
As we sit down by the fire.

Her dad is a famous lawyer
Who works with all the stars,
He's always jetting off round the world
And buying expensive cars.

Her mum is a High Court judge,
She's really made it big,
Sitting there in the courtroom
In her long white curly wig.

Tracey tells them about her dad's yacht
And their other house in Spain,
Mum starts to call her 'love' and 'dear'
And says she really must come again.

THOUGHTS IN THE DENTIST'S WAITING ROOM

Sitting in the temple of doom,
That's called the dentist's waiting room.
Well-thumbed mags are all around,
The air is filled with a chilling sound,
Like a council workman he's doing his drilling,
I wonder if I'll need a filling?
Or perhaps a couple of painful extractions?
I wish I was in school doing my fractions!
Or running a long cross-country race,
I wonder if I'll need a brace?
Please God, do you think we could make a deal?
I'll promise never to lie or steal,
Cheat or swear or moan or fight,
And I'll do my homework every night.
I'll give up chocolate, lollies and sweets,
Gum and sherbet, all kinds of treats.
I'll brush my teeth twice every day,
So they glint and gleam and don't decay.
I'll keep my bedroom tidy all the time
And hang the washing out on the line.
We'll take it further, I've thought of another,
I'll even be nice to my little brother!
The door finally opens, I'm filled with dread,
Couldn't someone else go in instead?
Please, it's not my turn, there's been an error,
My legs won't move, paralysed with terror.
I cower in the chair not making a sound,
Gleaming tools are all around.
No one can know how bad I feel,
Remember God, have we got a deal?

TREVOR JONES

Trevor Jones
Had elastic bones
And trembled like a jelly.
Chocolate and sweets
And all manner of treats
Had swelled his bulging belly.

He joined a gym
In a bid to get thin,
But the coach thought he was a chump,
Until he bounced one day,
And the coach gasped 'I say,
This boy can really jump!'

Trev sweated and strained,
He worked and trained,
'Til he was really one of the best.
Then one day it came,
His chance for fame,
He strained for the ultimate test.

Olympic delight!
As he jumped like a kite,
Heading for worldwide glory,
As the crowd roared,
And Trevor soared,
Things turned a little gory.

There were creaks and groans
From his elastic bones
As Trevor went zap and zoom.
He split in two,
As he sped and flew,
And whizzed off past the moon.

Now Astronomers gaze
Through night-time haze,
Tracing him through the sky.
They watch Trev's comet
As it zooms like a rocket
And wave as it flashes by!

WELLINGTON

His fur is deepest, darkest midnight,
Peppered with silver stars,
A warrior cat, a fighting cat,
Covered with battle scars.

Lolling in the flickering firelight,
That glows on pink padded paws
So gentle and baby soft, but concealing
Deadly, razor-like claws.

A distant noise disturbs him,
Saucer eyes scan and glare,
His teeth are pearly mousetraps,
Primed and prepared.

A tongue-like coarse, dry sandpaper,
Licking fur like the finest silk,
Soon purrs like a contented pneumatic drill,
Dreaming of his morning milk.

THE SCHOOL PHOTOGRAPH

Today is the school photograph
And I've got a big red spot.
I've also got a little brother,
Cheers, God, thanks a lot.

Our photo will be taken together
As if we're the best of mates,
When really he's number one
On the list of things I hate.

I'll have to make sure he looks okay,
Like a normal human being.
So the photographer doesn't know
Quite what a monster she is seeing.

He'll have something round his mouth
Like you really wouldn't believe,
And his runny nose'll need wiping,
If he hasn't done it on his sleeve.

There'll be something down his jumper
That'd baffle scientists in a lab,
Just for the photo couldn't I swap him
For one of the other lads?

I'll have to brush his scarecrow hair,
A knotted, tangly mop,
And when his finger's up his nose,
I'll loudly tell him, 'Stop!'

Now it's three weeks later
And the photos have all come,
My brother is handsomely smiling
Like I'm his dearest, bestest chum.

The thing that really spoils it,
The thing that's really grot,
Is that looking, big and red and round,
Is my massive, horrid spot!

THE SCHOOL PHOTOGRAPH

Today is the school photograph,
Which alone is bad enough,
But I've also got a big sister,
Life can be really tough.

Our photo will be taken together,
It'll end up on the wall,
But the person with my sister
Won't look like me at all.

'Cos my sister has got orders
To make me look like a handsome duke,
And we've been told to smile so sweetly,
It makes me want to puke!

She'll straighten my grotty, twisted tie
And carefully comb my hair.
She'll wipe my nose and tut a lot,
My mates are gonna stare.

Then she'll lick a yucky tissue
And wipe all round my face,
Moaning all the time she's doing it,
Until she hasn't left a trace.

Every year when the photos come back
My parents groan 'Oh Dan!'
They say my sister looks so lovely
And I'm like the Hunchback of Notre Dame.

Now it's three weeks later
And the photos have all come,
It doesn't look like me at all
And I'm not going to get done.

But the thing that really makes it great,
That really lifts the gloom,
Is that my sister has a huge red spot
And now she's crying in her room.

MY FAVOURITE TEACHER (NOT)

Mr Jones storms into the room,
Daily filling our hearts with gloom,
With gnashing teeth, all bad and yellowing,
And a thunderous roar, loud and bellowing,
He shushes us like an angry viper,
With the precision of an enemy sniper,
Then longer, like a kettle boiling,
He's not happy until we're all toiling.
He walks round the room with a positive swagger,
His tongue as deadly as a murderer's dagger,
And a temper as fast as an Olympic sprinter,
His voice is a sliver of icy winter.
Inside my brain I suffer so much pain,
Like fingernails on the blackboard, again and again.
And I'd like to go to the Court of Human Rights
About the homework he sets us on Friday nights.
Yes, I love Mr Jones's lessons such a lot
And he's my very favourite teacher (not!).

PLEASE COME HOME, MUM

Mum's been in hospital,
She's been there for eight days,
She's coming out tomorrow,
I hope with no delays.

I suppose you'd say Dad's struggled,
Though really he's done his best,
But the kitchen's really untidy
And the lounge is truly messed.

The plants have really suffered,
All but two are dead,
And if it wasn't for the takeaway,
I don't think we'd've been fed.

When Dad has tried to cook
I can't tell you how bad it's been,
Burnt saucepans are littered everywhere,
The kitchen looks really obscene.

Yesterday he made disgusting porridge
That was horribly thick and lumpy.
Then when his mates invited him down the pub
He couldn't - so he got all grumpy.

Is Dad allergic to the washing machine?
'Cos he hasn't turned it on,
And the utility room looks like it's been hit
By a massive nuclear bomb.

There's my school uniform on the floor
And my PE kit all mucky,
And the smell of Dad's mangy socks
Filling the air is yucky.

We just can't stand another day,
Please save us from our fate,
So please come home tomorrow, Mum,
We really just can't wait.

JANUARY

Dreary days and dreary times,
Wet washing on washing lines.
Wind like a razor, slicing deep,
The homeless shiver in dreamless sleep.
Dawn breaks, desolate gloom,
Iced windows in dismal rooms.
Late risers, cocooned in beds,
Buttoned blazers, bobble-hatted heads,
Numbed noses, numbed toes,
Milky sun weakly glows.
Abandoned dog, shivering, feeble,
The cold pierces like a needle.
Smoking chimneys, dragon breath,
Freezing birds facing death.
Frozen toes on frozen feet,
Bleached, cheerless, monochrome street.

THE CROCODILE

When you see the crocodile at the zoo,
Remember too that he sees you.
With razor teeth and beady-eye,
He watches every passer-by.
Quiet and calm and still and sly,
He's waiting for a girl or boy,
To fall for his smiling, trusty grin
And put their hand close to him.
Then quick as lightning, snap, snap, snap,
He'll eat the silly little chap.
Skin and bones and flesh and fat,
Just you all remember that!

LOOKING AFTER NEXT DOOR'S CATS WHILE THEY ARE ON HOLIDAY

There's cat sick on the patio
And dead mice in the hall,
There's a funny smell in the lounge
That I don't recognise at all.

There's scratches on the lino
And they've been digging up the plants,
I think Tabitha needs the vet,
She won't eat and just lies there and pants.

I start to think I've lost Henry,
Which would be a real nightmare,
I think of death on a big busy road,
Then he's sitting there on the stair.

Marmalade has caught a bird
After hours of climbing trees,
And a quick look at Joshua shows
He's covered in hopping fleas.

Horatio doesn't like me,
He lounges there and stares,
Later I find he's been moulting
And the settee is covered in hairs.

Finally I manage to trace the pong
But it really fails to amuse,
As one of the lovely pussy cats
Has made a mess in my shoes.

I just hope I get through to next Saturday
Without too many awful scares,
And no more sick down me nails,
I'll start to say me prayers.

And next year I'll have to be smarter,
So I don't have to suffer this pain,
I'll find out when they're going
And quickly book my week in Spain.

TODAY DOWN MY STREET...

'It's time for breakfast, Tom, come on before it gets cold.'
    'But, Mum, Superman's coming down our street
    With Batman
    And they've just passed a bus!'
'Just hurry up!'
    'But now there's Mickey Mouse
    Being chased by Top Cat
    And he's being chased by a big spotty dog!'
'Oh, come on!'
    'Mum, there's an enormous crocodile
    After an eighty-eight-year-old lady.
    But it's okay, a policeman in shorts is coming!'
'Tom!'
    'A three-eyed alien is talking
    With Paddington and Rupert
    And a rhino and a giant flower and . . .'
'But, Tom, you know the London Marathon goes past our house,
And your breakfast is getting cold!'

CHRISTMAS JOY

Misty windows, TV flickering,
Christmas time, families bickering,
Aunts and uncles round for lunch,
Yucky sprouts for all to munch;
Too much food in bulging bellies,
Lots of repeats on people's tellies;
In the New Year, Mum starts her diet,
After the arguments all goes quiet;
Empty bottles, Dad's been boozing,
Now he's snoring while he's snoozing;
Santa left presents in the early morning,
An exciting day, but kids are yawning;
Playing up, they're overtired,
Some early nights will be required;
They've reached day's end, baubles shining,
But at least there is a silver lining;
Another whole year 'til they have to eat sprouts,
'Time for bed!' Dad tiredly shouts.

HENRIETTA HENRY

The Robinson family: Mum and Dad,
With sister Susie and Henry the lad,
Decided they'd go to somewhere new,
So off they went, down to the zoo.
They saw the monkeys in their cages,
Dad bought ice creams with his wages,
It was then the trouble really started
When Henry, from his family, he was parted.
Henry was a monstrous little devil
Who liked to mess and muddle and meddle,
To drive his teachers to their wit's end
And send his parents round the bend.
It wasn't long before he caused some stress,
He didn't half get in a mess!
He fed wine gums to the pandas,
Stuck out his tongue at the salmandas,
Pulled monstrous faces at the chimps,
And called the baboons a bunch of wimps.
He frightened the parrots in their cages,
The noise and fuss went on for ages.
He shouted 'Fatty!' at the hippo so mountainous
And 'Big nose!' at the elephant so fountainous.
Finally he went right off the rails
And tried to pull the lions' tails.
Among the lions with mouths all cavernous
Stood one who was especially ravenous,
This fierce lion called Henrietta
Decided she'd like nothing better
Than to have a boy for her dinner-time treat,
Head and body and legs and feet.
She started promptly to do just that
And quickly ate the little chap.
She gobbled him up with a chew and a slurp
And finally gave out a great big burp!

The moral of this story, we must conclude,
Is that we shouldn't be mischievous or rude,
When at the zoo we should act nicely
And do as we are told, precisely.
Otherwise Henrietta might one day munch,
On you or me for her lunch.

YOU'RE NOT GOING OUT DRESSED LIKE THAT!

You're not going out dressed like that!
What will the neighbours say?
What will my friends say?
What will Dad say?
Just look at yourself in the mirror.
You can't wear all that make-up
And your skirt's too short,
Anyway, orange isn't your colour
And it doesn't go with red.
Those heels are ridiculous.
It's cold out
And you haven't got a coat,
And what have you done to your hair?
No, there's not a chance,
You're not going out dressed like that, Mum.

SCHOOL REPORT

Mum rips open the dreaded brown envelope
And as usual they've got it all wrong,
My teachers just don't understand me,
I don't think that I'm going to live long!

In History, Geography, Maths and Art,
My teachers aren't very impressed,
Mum's face frowns more with every line,
I'm beginning to feel depressed!

I must concentrate fully 'cos I'm easily put off,
In French my accent is weak,
My handwriting's hard to decipher,
My holiday plans start to look bleak!

In Science I display a lack of understanding,
My homework is too untidy and too late,
This isn't quite what I'd hoped for,
My father is planning my fate!

Overall my progress is disappointing
And my future, it seems, depends
Upon displaying a more positive attitude
And not showing off quite so much to my friends!

Visions of extra tuition
Dance menacingly through my poor head,
Perhaps the solution could be relaxation,
Chocolate, sweets and ice creams instead?

But reality returns as the last page is read
And the torture has finally ended,
My father tuts as he announces my fate,
'Son, you're indefinitely grounded?'

So next year I'm going to try harder
To keep my head down and not shirk,
That's what I've promised them anyway,
After they both went completely berserk!

DETENTION!

Monday
'Why are you late, Smith?'
'Well . . .
I was getting up, well on time, and a slithery, slimy, boggle-eyed alien from the planet Zarb appeared and refused to let me go until I gave him my mum's recipe for spaghetti bolognaise.'
'Right - detention!'

Tuesday
'Why are you late, Smith?'
'Well . . .
As I was walking to school, well on time you understand, I saw a bank robber running down the street. I tripped him up and then me and a big fat granny sat on him 'til the police arrived. They said, I'll get a reward.'
'Right - detention!'

Wednesday
'Why are you late, Smith?'
'Well . . .
I was about to come out of the house, with oodles of time of course, when I heard gurgles from the downstairs loo. My little brother had got his head stuck and it was filling up, and he was drowning. So I stuck a hose-pipe in his mouth so he could breathe and dialled 999. They said I'd saved his life.'
'Right - detention!'

Thursday
'Why are you late, Smith?'
'Well . . .
I was up in plenty of time when there was a knock on the door and, well, you remember the slithery, slimy, boggle-eyed alien from Monday? Well, him and his mates liked the recipe so much that they took me for a slap-up meal in a restaurant on the planet Zarb and I took my camera to prove there is life in outer space.'
'Right - detention!'

Friday
'Why are you late, Smith?'
'Well . . .
I was dressed and ready, in very good time as always, when a TV crew knocked at my door and wanted to interview me about all the heroic things I've done this week and that took ages, especially when they saw my photo, and now they want to speak to you, sir.'
'Right - delighted to meet you. Oh yes, young Martin is a fine pupil, so keen, he often stays behind after school . . .'

THE SCHOOL NURSE IS COMING TODAY

The school nurse is coming today
To jab that terrible, sharp needle deep into my arm,
Spread panic and fear and woe all around
And generally do me harm.

She'll smile so sweetly while we wait in line,
But to us her mission's plain,
To make us sweat, awaiting our turn
And cause us maximum pain.

She must get a strange job satisfaction,
Her customers all quaking with dread,
Shoving her sharp needle deep into our veins
And dispensing cotton wool to dab on when it's bled.

We all try to change the subject
And tell jokes to lift the gloom,
But each one of us secretly knows
That we must face our personal doom.

We must try hard to remain very macho,
And pretend we don't care and we ain't
Worried about needles or blood or the pain
Or being the one, this year, to faint.

Finally we're called for, the game is up,
Each one of us prays for delay,
But we all take our place in that fearsome line 'cos
The school nurse has come today.

NAPOLEON

Ginger tomcat,
Napoleon,
Basks in
Afternoon sunshine.
Lazily surveys
His kingdom.
Glossy coat,
Padded paws,
Contempt for all.
S-T-R-E-T-C-H-E-S.
Purrs a while.
Soon asleep.
Summer's day
Drifts away . . .

HALF-TIME

I like to sip my steaming Bovril
As I sit in the stand at half-time,
And moan how the centre forward's
Not as good as I was in my prime.
How they prance around like ballerinas
And roll around like a fairy when hurt
And how if I was twenty years younger
I could be wearing that number nine shirt.
Our centre forward really is a nightmare,
I can't believe they've paid such a fee
For a player who misses chance after chance,
When for a small sum, they could've had me.
I dream how I'd lead them out,
Glance up for a moment, and look round,
With a capacity crowd packed inside,
Chanting my name all round the ground.
So I write a small note to the manager
As I wait for the second half to start,
That says next time we need a centre forward
Look for my ad in Exchange and Mart.

THE ELEPHANT AND THE ENGINEER

One Sunday morning something quite queer
Happened to a civil engineer,
An elephant came from Timbuktu
And said, 'I want to live with you.'

'Please step inside, sir, please explain,
How came you here, by train or plane?
By boat or raft across the sea?
Step inside, sir, sit down please.'

They talked in the conservatory,
And Mr Elephant retold his story,
'I've left my home, I've lost my friends,
I really am at my wit's end.'

The engineer didn't know what to do,
But kindness in the end shone through.
He said, 'You can stay,' with apprehension,
'But I'll have to build a big extension.'

An architect friend drew up the plan,
But that was where the problems began.
The engineer said, 'All may be lost,
I don't think I can afford the cost.'

He asked about a government grant,
He said he'd a pet elephant,
The clerk said, 'I'm sorry, but no,
I can't think where you could go.'

He asked the bank manager for a loan,
But he said, 'No,' by telephone.
Then excitedly he began to squeal,
'I know, we'll hold a public appeal!'

'We'll ask the people to give a donation,
To pay for Mr Elephant's habitation,
A penny here, a shilling there,
This is the answer to my prayer.'

Adverts were placed in the local paper,
Posters were hung with paste and stapler,
Engineer and elephant were on the news,
Churchgoers prayed for them in the pews.

But an elephant in town did not amuse
The mayor who said he'd eat his shoes
If he couldn't get rid of the enormous beast
With trunk and tusks and skin all creased.

He took the elephant to court
Where a legal battle was fiercely fought.
Witnesses were called and closely questioned,
The Prime Minister was interested, someone mentioned.

On the final day they had a break for lunch
And the mayor went out for something to munch.
After a lovely meal he felt all was fine,
'Til his car stopped dead on the railway line!

Then a train came zooming round the bend,
The mayor thought this really was the end.
He closed his eyes in dismay,
All hope gone, he started to pray.

All of a sudden, he started to move,
It was quick and bumpy, not very smooth.
The express train missed him and rushed by,
The mayor raised his eyes in thanks to the sky.

All he could see was an enormous beast
With trunk and tusks and skin all creased.
The answer had come to his prayer,
Mr Elephant, he had saved the mayor!

They sped back to court, but they were late,
Judge and jury were deciding his fate.
The outcome no one dared to predict
The judge stood to read the verdict.

In the courtroom everyone held their breath,
It was silent, as quiet as death,
The judge opened his mouth to announce elephant's fate,
When in rushed the mayor and shouted, 'Wait!'

He whispered long in the judge's ear
Until finally the judge said, 'It does appear
That all opposition to the elephant has now gone away,
And so, Mr Elephant, he can stay.'

The crowd stood and started to applaud,
Then shouted and whooped, cheered and roared,
The newspapers interviewed him so that all could read
About Mr Elephant's daring deed.

There was a grand party at the Town Hall
So the people of the town could all
Welcome Mr Elephant to their town,
And help him, at last, to settle down.

Now, Mr Elephant, he has settled well
And has his own house in a dingly dell,
And in the summer the big grey mountain
Works outside the court, as a fountain.

THE CREATURE

After a dreamless sleep,
The beast
Is coaxed
Into life.
It stirs,
Seemingly sniffing
The chill morning air.
Groaning and shivering,
Shuddering in the gloom,
Its tough skin,
Encrusted with frost.
It coughs and splutters,
Suddenly
Opens white,
Staring,
Piercing eyes.
Roars!
Producing steamy bad breath.
Its heart
Pumps alien blood
Around its frozen body.
The creature
Grows angrier
And lurches painfully.
Then nothing . . .
The eyes fade,
The heart stops
And it breathes no more.
Time for regret?
Time for tears?
No!
Time to walk to school.
Why do I always rely
On Dad's old car?

THE NEW BOY

They jumped to conclusions about the new lad
And called him names just because he was new,
They bullied and baited and teased him
'Cos it gave them something to do.

His ways were somewhat different,
Like when an aeroplane swooped and rushed by,
He ran to the window, shouted and waved
And then stared, 'til it was gone from the sky.

His hair was knotted and straggly,
Like spaghetti gone out of control,
He drew pictures of strange people and places
And stared at the fish in their bowl!

When Miss called him a little monster
Or said his work was out of this world,
A smile spread over his face and we saw
His long teeth and his tongue all curled.

His voice didn't sound like he was from round here,
And he'd been taught a funny way to write,
He spent an awful lot of time stargazing
With his telescope, late at night.

Then one day he just didn't turn up
But he'd left me a goodbye letter
Saying, 'Please will you be my penpal 'cos
I've never met anyone better.'

At once I began to understand,
But the others thought he'd lost the plot,
'Cos on a map of the universe he'd plotted his home
And written, 'X marks the spot.'

So don't jump to conclusions about new lads
And call them names just because they're new,
Their ways are just slightly different
And at first glance they're not quite like you.

WIZZELDA WITCH

Wizzelda Witch, wicked and scary,
Lives with her cat, black and hairy,
In a cave, dark and deep,
Making spells, while children sleep.
Her cauldron splutters and steams and stews,
Making her potions, and making her brews.
It might seem strange and it might seem queer,
But she only goes out just once a year.
Then wearing her hat and her pitch-black clothes,
Laughing and cackling, with a wart on her nose,
Out of the window on her broomstick she rides,
Rockets and whizzes, speeds and glides.
Using her powers and potions and rhymes,
Evil she does, hundreds of times.
But soon it is light and night time has passed,
And Wizzelda is home, her last spell is cast.
You know I cannot promise, and I cannot be certain,
But just one night a year, pull back the curtain,
And up by the moon, there could be, just might,
Wizzelda Witch, on Hallowe'en Night.

STEVEN STATION

Steven Station in my class
Has met Rudolph and St Nicholas,
The Prime Minister pops round for his tea,
With kings and queens, one, two, three.

He's been to Africa and Egypt too,
And even has a pet gnu,
He drives a bright red racing motor
And comes to school by helicopter.

He jets his rocket to the stars
To play football with his friends from Mars,
He owns every toy that has been made,
And there's nothing of which he is afraid.

Don't get me wrong, I like the boy,
He daily fills our class with joy,
But really I think that Steven Station
Has the most vivid imagination!

THE HUNT

You are a fox,
The hunt is close behind,
Horns and hooves,
The yapping of hounds.
Your legs are tired
And you are breathing hard.
You have been chased up hills,
Across streams,
Through woodland,
Your fur ripped by barbed wire.
But you must go on,
A last, desperate effort.
The hooves shake the ground,
The barking is close.
You feel their hot breath.
You are filled with fear,
Helplessness.
Hopelessness,
They are upon you.
Savage teeth rip and tear,
Then nothing . . .

MR SNAIL

Mr Snail moves from place to place
At a microscopic dawdling pace,
While everywhere that he does roam,
He takes his own mobile home.
All day this gypsy mollusc slides,
'Til at day's end he skulks and hides.
From the Frenchman who believes his fate
Is to meet Mr Snail on his plate.
But these tiny creatures are not fools
Mr Snail would love to win the pools,
Then he would travel near and far
In a bright red racing motorcar,
Or he could retire by the sea,
Oh, how happy he would be!
But best of all he would like
To cross the Channel late one night,
And creep up on that Frenchman, Frank,
Driving his own chieftain tank!
Then Mr Snail could tell that bully that he
Now eats greedy Frenchmen for his tea.

STRAY

Discarded.
Alone and frightened.
Sharp ribs revealed
Through matted fur.
A forgotten outcast,
Rejected and outlawed.
Shunned,
Like a leper of old,
For an unknown crime.
Skulks hungrily,
In search of refuge.
Craves
A warm bed
And kind hands.
Cringes.
Shivers sadly,
In the drizzle.
Sleeping rough
In the pet shop doorway
Where 'kind' owners
Once befriended him.

LIFE'S A SPOT ON YOUR NOSE

You've asked her out
After weeks of fretting,
She's turned you down,
It's so upsetting.
Life's a spot on your nose!

You look in the mirror,
Things just don't look right,
Your face is lopsided,
Like you've just lost a fight.
Life's a spot on your nose!

You've done your homework
And it's been eaten by the mice,
You used that excuse last week,
It certainly won't work twice.
Life's a spot on your nose!

You're late for school,
The third time this week,
Mr Jones'll be much
Too cross to speak.
Life's a spot on your nose!

You look again in the mirror
Before you go out to the disco.
It can't be, not now,
You start to go psycho,
A big red spot on your nose!

I LEARNT TO SWIM AT THE MUNICIPAL BATHS

I learnt to swim
At the municipal baths
But now they're tearing it down.
Chlorine and noise,
Being one of the boys,
Bricks crash all around.

I swam my width
And everyone cheered;
Memories rush to my brain,
Echoes of friendships,
Ghosts reappear
As the bulldozer turns again.

Grumpy lifeguards;
We took the mick,
Fooling and larking around.
The crashing stops,
The dust drops,
All now razed to the ground.

WHY?

Why are things I like so bad for me?
And things I hate so good?
And why don't I like to eat the things
That doctors say I should?

Why do chocolate, ice cream, chips and treats,
Sugar, sweets and cake,
Make me big and fat and round
And make my stomach shake?

Why do they make my teeth all black
And wobble and fall out?
And make the dentist fret and frown?
It makes me want to shout!

They say you are what you eat,
And that girls are of sugar and spice,
But this doesn't really make much sense,
They can't have it their way twice!

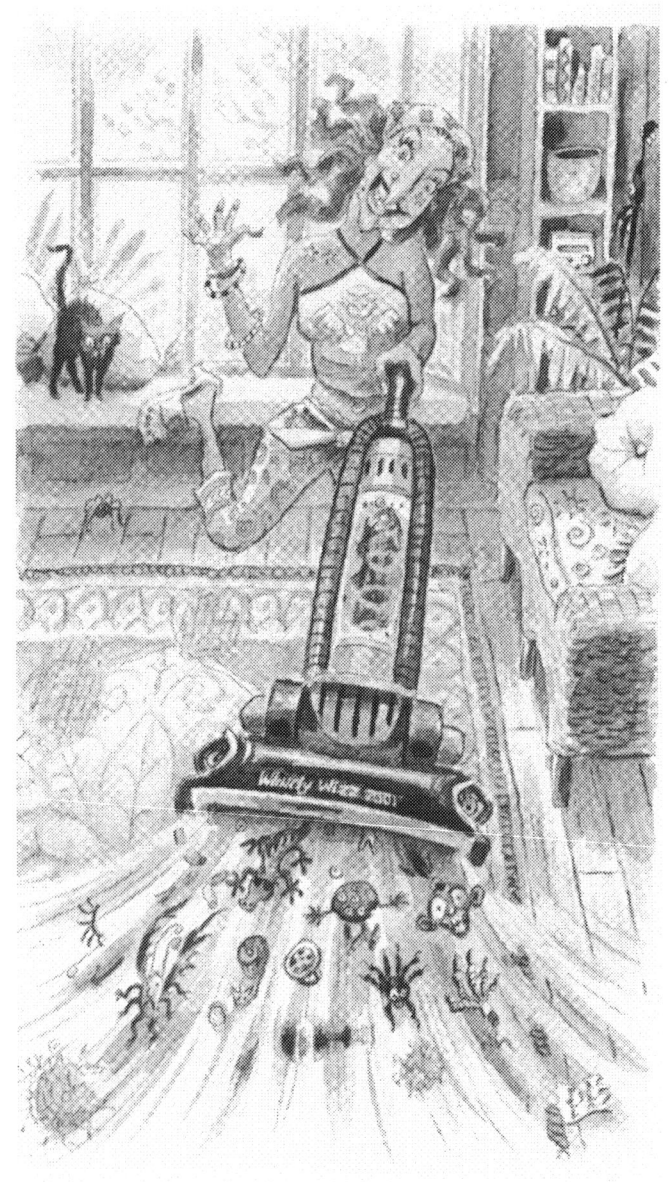

THE MODERN WITCH

The modern witch has sold her cave
And bought a semi in Belgrade.
Her broomstick redundant in the corner,
She flies by Concorde, cleans by hoover.
Her cauldron to a jumble sale she gave,
Now does cordon bleu by microwave.
She no longer wears her pitch-black clothes,
But down to Tammy Girl she goes.
Her wicked ways now given up,
She's even burnt her old spell book.
A good citizen now at the double,
No more 'Hubble, bubble, toil and trouble.'

SHIP AHOY!

Brave pirate captain, patch on eye,
Gives the shout, 'Ship Ahoy!'
His crew prepare without fear,
Each one a fierce buccaneer.

Jolly Roger flutters from the mast,
Crew are ready, canons blast!
Pistols fire and cutlasses dash,
Punches are thrown, bodies crash.

Soon all is quiet, the battle won,
Sea dogs celebrate, drinking rum.
The captain's eye glints with pleasure
As greedy hands share out the treasure.

MONDAY, 9.15AM

It's lesson one on Monday
With the dreaded Miss Spittlebottom,
Who treats me like something slimy
That crawled from under a rock.
But my mind soon starts to drift . . .
To the weekend
When playing out seemed
Much more fun than homework,
When playing footie came first
And learning my tables
And revising for my test
Never quite managed to even come second.
I remember the picture I drew
Of Miss Spittlebottom
With horns,
Bulging eyes like hard-boiled eggs,
Glasses
And a moustache,
And I recall the rude names
I called her to Dad,
And him saying she sounds
Like an evil old witch.
Suddenly
I realise the class is silent
And Miss Spittlebottom is staring at me.
A thought hits me like
A whack from a cold, wet haddock . . .
If Dad's right
And she's a witch,
Can she read my mind?

ANGER

My anger
Is like a big red balloon
Being pumped up,
S-T-R-A-I-N-I-N-G,
S-T-R-E-T-C-H-I-N-G.
How could he say that?
Why did they do it?
It isn't fair!
No, not homework for the weekend?
Why do I have to go to bed?
Why can't I go?
When will I be old enough?
My friends are allowed to,
Why can't I?
Why do I have to have sensible shoes?
My music isn't too loud!
Why can't I have my hair cut like that?
Arrrrrrrr!
It's not fair!
The balloon finally bursts . . .